God's
DAILY
ANSWER

devotions to renew your soul

for Teachers

God's
DAILY
ANSWER

devotions to renew your soul

for Teachers

*G*od is inscrutable—there will always be aspects of His person we aren't capable of understanding. He knows our need for answers, and has responded by giving us the Scriptures, rich oral traditions, and the witness of our hearts to let us know what we can expect from Him, how He wishes to interact with us, and the various aspects of His character. He encourages us to ask and seek, and when we do, He assures us we will find.

As a teacher, you undoubtedly field questions from your students on a daily basis, and you almost certainly have questions of your own. That's why we designed *God's Daily Answer for Teachers*. As you read, you will gain a God's-eye view about common issues like relationships, finances, work, and forgiveness. We hope you will also come to know more intimately the One who holds *all* the answers—the One who holds you in the palm of His hand.

Table of Contents

God's Love	10
Finances	12
Wisdom	14
Goals	16
Humor	18
Growth	20
Speech	22
Work	24
Fresh Start	26
Nature	28
Thankfulness	30
Character	32
Enthusiasm	34
Gentleness	36
Determination	38
Joy	40
Prayer	42
Health	44
Rest	46
Love	48
Relationships	50
Justice	52
Priorities	54
Patience	56

Time	58
Faith	60
Peace	62
Hope	64
Trust	66
Friendship	68
Strength	70
Motivation	72
Integrity	74
Contentment	76
Learning	78
Grace	80
Compassion	82
Gifts and Talents	84
Wealth	86
Confidence	88
Future	90
Blessings	92
Loyalty	94
Mercy	96
Security	98
God's Faithfulness	100
Thoughts	102
Eternal Life	104
Forgiveness	106

Life	108
Success	110
Scripture	112
Responsibility	114
Comfort	116
Satisfaction	118
Courage	120
Expectancy	122
Humility	124
Generosity	126
Decisions	128
Meditation	130
Goodness	132
Protection	134
Encouragement	136
Identity	138
God's Forgiveness	140
Honesty	142
Perseverance	144
Faithfulness	146
Kindness	148
Guidance	150
Fun	152
Preparation	154

Teaching is a partnership with God.

You are not molding iron nor chiseling marble;
you are working with the Creator of the universe
in shaping human character and
determining destiny.

RUTH VAUGHN

God's Love

*God's love has been poured into our hearts through
the Holy Spirit that has been given to us.*

ROMANS 5:5 NRSV

The Scriptures say God is love. He is the essence of it, the fulfillment of it, the source of it. When you come to know Him, you are the recipient of that great and boundless ocean of love.

Never again will you feel no one cares for you. Your Creator cares. Never again will you wonder if His love for you will end. God has promised that nothing—absolutely nothing—can separate you from His love. Never again will you ask yourself if your life has value. As the object of God's unlimited love, you are of great value.

Carry that love with you as you walk into your classroom each morning, and give your students a sample of what real love—God's love—is all about.

———✦——— ———✦——— ———✦———

Jesus did not come to make God's love possible,
but to make God's love visible.

AUTHOR UNKNOWN

God's love is always supernatural,
always a miracle,
always the last thing we deserve.

ROBERT HORN

God soon turns from his wrath,
but he never turns from his love.

CHARLES HADDON SPURGEON

Every existing thing is equally upheld
in its existence by God's creative love.

SIMONE WEIL

God proves his love for us in that
while we still were sinners Christ died for us.

ROMANS 5:8 NRSV

Finances

My God will fully satisfy every need of yours according to his riches in glory in Christ Jesus.

PHILIPPIANS 4:19 NRSV

You probably didn't become a teacher with the idea of getting rich. Most people who decide to spend their lives in a classroom have answered a higher calling. But the initial desire to teach can become buried under a mountain of anxiety about bills and making ends meet. It can make you resent your calling. A lot of teachers leave the profession to find higher paying jobs.

If you are staying the course, you should take courage in the fact God knows your needs. You can count on Him to provide unique ways to supplement your income, and creative ideas for living within your means. He's called you to have a hand in shaping the next generation. You do your part, and He will do His.

If a person gets his attitude toward money straight, it will help straighten out almost every other area in his life.

BILLY GRAHAM

Money has never yet made anyone rich.

SENECA

There is no portion of money that is our money
and the rest God's money. It is all his; he made it
all, gives it all, and he has simply trusted it
to us for his service. A servant has two purses,
the master's and his own, but we have only one.

ADOLPHE MONOD

Use everything as if it belongs to God.
It does. You are his steward.

AUTHOR UNKNOWN

Keep your lives free from the love of money
and be satisfied with what you have,
because God has said, "I will never leave you;
I will never forget you."

HEBREWS 13:5 NCV

Wisdom

*If any of you is lacking in wisdom, ask God,
who gives to all generously and ungrudgingly,
and it will be given you.*

JAMES 1:5 NRSV

Every teacher has encountered that bright, promising student who refuses to complete assignments and doesn't seem to listen. Despite your best efforts, your grade book is filled with incompletes. How can you break through?

Pray for wisdom as you search for ways to motivate that gifted student. It may be an idea for stimulating a natural curiosity or the development of a unique approach to the information. Every child is different. But God knows each child's specific needs. He can help you find an angle when no one else can.

God has gifted you with the talents and skills you need to do the job He's called you to do. Turn to Him often for wisdom and insight.

Wisdom is a gift direct from God.

BOB JONES

Wisdom is concerned with how we relate to people, to the world, and to God.

EDMUND P. CLOWNEY

Wisdom is knowledge rightly applied.

AUTHOR UNKNOWN

Knowledge comes, but wisdom lingers.

ALFRED LORD TENNYSON

The LORD gives wisdom; from his mouth come knowledge and understanding.

PROVERBS 2:6 NRSV

Goals

Forgetting what lies behind and straining forward to what lies ahead, I press on toward the goal for the prize of the heavenly call of God in Christ Jesus.

PHILIPPIANS 3:13–14 NRSV

Goal-setting is an important part of every teacher's preparation for the school year. First, those goals the school district mandates must be acknowledged and merged with your own. Then, you must structure your lesson plans and study units to conform with them. By the time school begins, you're ready to begin the process of achieving the best possible outcome.

In the frenetic pace of a new school year, however, it's easy to forget the most important goal of all—growing closer to God. You will need His wisdom, His counsel, His inspiration, and so much more as you strive to educate and motivate your students. As you get to know Him and His values and priorities, you will sense a renewed purpose and inspiration in your teaching.

First build a proper goal. That proper goal will make it easy, almost automatic, to build a proper you.

JOHANN WOLFGANG VON GOETHE

The goal of a virtuous life is to become like God.

GREGORY OF NYSSA

You become successful the moment
you start moving toward a worthwhile goal.

AUTHOR UNKNOWN

Before you score, you just have a goal.

AUTHOR UNKNOWN

Our only goal is to please God.

2 CORINTHIANS 5:9 NCV

Humor

He will yet fill your mouth with laughter.

JOB 8:21 NASB

How often do you treat yourself to a good, old-fashioned belly laugh? Admittedly, teaching is an awesome responsibility, but it also provides plenty of material for potential laughs. Those laughs are good for you *and* your students.

It's easy to become focused on the cares of this world: the threat of terrorism, child predators, or violence in and around your school. You carry a burden for your students testing well and growing toward their potential. But that doesn't mean you have to do your job grim faced and somber.

And, consider this notable bonus: humor strengthens your immune system, making you more resistant to disease—never a bad idea with all those delightful germ-carriers around you every day.

Laughter adds richness, texture,
and color to otherwise ordinary days.
It is a gift, a choice, a discipline, and an art.

TIM HANSEL

Humor is the great thing, the saving thing. The minute it crops up, all our irritations and resentments slip away and a sunny spirit takes their place.

MARK TWAIN

True humor springs not more from the head than from the heart; it is not contempt, its essence is love.

THOMAS CARLYLE

Laughter is the most beautiful and beneficial therapy God ever granted humanity.

CHARLES R. SWINDOLL

A cheerful heart is good medicine.

PROVERBS 17:22 NRSV

Growth

*Neither the one who plants nor the one who waters
is anything, but only God who gives the growth.*

1 CORINTHIANS 3:7 NRSV

When you were a child or a young adult,
someone planted a seed in you—a desire
to grow and teach others what you had learned. That
seed of promise was watered by teachers, mentors,
family, or friends, and by your own dreams.

Now that you have become the "farmer," you
plant seeds of knowledge and hope in your students.
At the beginning of the school year, you patiently
water them for weeks before seeing the first signs
of growth. Then harvest comes at the end of the
season. But only God knows the rate at which each
seed will grow.

Growth takes time. Even though you are the
teacher now, you are still growing. Let God continue
to help you develop your abilities.

Be not afraid of growing slowly;
be afraid only of standing still.

CHINESE PROVERB

Gradual growth in grace, knowledge, faith, love,
holiness, humility, and spiritual-mindedness—
all this I see clearly taught and urged in Scripture.
But sudden, instantaneous leaps from conversion
to consecration, I fail to see in the Bible.

J. C. RYLE

Progress in the Christian life is exactly equal to
the growing knowledge we gain of
the Triune God in personal experience.

A. W. TOZER

If we don't change, we don't grow. If we don't
grow, we are not really living. Growth demands
a temporary surrender of security.

GAIL SHEEHY

Grow in the grace and knowledge of our Lord
and Savior Jesus Christ.

2 PETER 3:18 NCV

Speech

Let your speech always be with grace.

COLOSSIANS 4:6 NASB

A childhood saying goes, "Sticks and stones may break my bones, but words will never hurt me." But, words do hurt. They can destroy confidence and self-esteem.

In your classroom, you have a wide range of students who have grown up in homes with varying kinds of speech—some peppered with curse words, some poisoned with anger, and some filled with love and encouragement. You have an opportunity to use your words to heal and reinforce.

Children need encouragement, secure boundaries, and firm discipline. Listen to the words you speak to them. Are they filled with grace—God's unmerited favor?

Kind words produce their image on men's souls;
and a beautiful image it is. They smooth,
and quiet, and comfort the hearer.

BLAISE PASCAL

It is easier to look wise than to talk wisely.

SAINT AMBROSE

Good words are worth much and cost little.

GEORGE HERBERT

Speaking without thinking is shooting
without aiming.

SIR WILLIAM GURNEY BENHAM

When you talk, do not say harmful things.
But say what people need—words that will help
others become stronger.

EPHESIANS 4:29 NCV

Work

The LORD recompense thy work,
and a full reward be given thee.

RUTH 2:12 KJV

No one will ever know all the preparation and unseen work you put into your job. No one, that is, but God.

He watched over you when you stayed up late studying for your final exams in college. Now He gives you the strength to get up early or stay up late grading papers and preparing lesson plans. He gives you the confidence you need to stand before your students and answer their questions.

You may not receive the accolades of parents, or hear the applause of your peers every day, but God will reward you for your labor in teaching and nurturing your students. Your work matters to Him. That's ultimately what makes it worth doing.

―――――――――――――――

I long to accomplish a great and noble task;
but it is my chief duty to accomplish small tasks
as if they were great and noble.

HELEN KELLER

Far and away the best prize that life offers is
the chance to work hard at work worth doing.

THEODORE ROOSEVELT

All good work is done the way ants do things,
little by little.

LAFCADIO HEARN

Work becomes worship when done for the Lord.

AUTHOR UNKNOWN

*Be steadfast, immovable, always excelling in
the work of the Lord, because you know that in
the Lord your labor is not in vain.*

1 CORINTHIANS 15:58 NRSV

Fresh Start

*You have begun to live the new life, in which
you are being made new and are becoming like
the One who made you.*

COLOSSIANS 3:10 NCV

Spending all day in a classroom is stressful.
As the day wears on, you may find yourself
snapping at a student, rather than taking the time
to give a thoughtful response; or going home and
unloading on the first family member who crosses
your path.

When that happens, God is eager to forgive you,
and help you forgive yourself, so you can get back to
doing the job He's called you to do. He knows that
every moment you spend in guilt and recrimination
will be a moment lost—a moment that will not be
spent influencing the lives of others.

When you know you've blown it, go to God
without hesitation. He will help you make it right
and give you a fresh, new start.

I like sunrises, Mondays, and new seasons.
God seems to be saying, "With me you can
always start afresh."

ADA LUM

If you have made mistakes, even serious ones,
there is always another chance for you.
What we call failure is not the falling down,
but the staying down.

MARY PICKFORD

With each sunrise, we start anew.

AUTHOR UNKNOWN

Each day is a new life. Seize it. Live it.

DAVID GUY POWERS

If anyone belongs to Christ, then he is made new.
The old things have gone; everything is made new!
All this is from God.

2 CORINTHIANS 5:17–18 NCV

Nature

You shall go out in joy, and be led back in peace;
the mountains and the hills before
you shall burst into song.

ISAIAH 55:12 NRSV

Are you enduring a season in your life when hope seems hard to find? Like winter in the Snow Belt, you look out the windows of your soul and see nothing but bare branches, and wonder whether this season will ever end.

If you're feeling tired and hopeless, find a place where you can enjoy God's nearness and see His awesome greatness in the things He has created. The yellow of the first daffodil, for example, can bring renewed hope that summer is just around the corner.

Maybe it's time to visit the nearest indoor botanical garden, or take a walk in the woods, where God can renew your soul. You'll be a better person and a better teacher after taking one of these inspirational breaks to enjoy God's gift of nature.

I love to think of nature as an unlimited broadcasting station through which God speaks to us every hour, if we will only tune in.

GEORGE WASHINGTON CARVER

The more I study nature,
the more I am amazed at the Creator.

LOUIS PASTEUR

Nature is but a name for an effect
whose cause is God.

WILLIAM COWPER

We can almost smell the aroma of God's beauty
in the fresh spring flowers. His breath
surrounds us in the warm summer breezes.

GALE HEIDE

*The heavens declare the glory of God;
and the firmament sheweth his handiwork.*

PSALM 19:1 KJV

Thankfulness

Always be thankful.

COLOSSIANS 3:15 TLB

In the middle of the school day when you're feeling most hard-pressed—that's the time to give God thanks. Begin by thanking Him for your students and the opportunities you've been given to make a difference in their lives. Then take a moment to look into their faces and give thanks for each one, especially those who cause the most disruption.

You will find that giving thanks for your students increases your appreciation for each one as God's totally unique creation. It's a reminder that even your most difficult student has been placed on this earth to fulfill a God-given destiny and is, therefore, precious in His eyes. God has given you an extraordinary privilege—helping His precious ones become all He intends them to be.

Thou has given so much to me.
Give me one thing more—a grateful heart.

GEORGE HERBERT

Thanksgiving is good but thanks-living is better.

MATTHEW HENRY

No duty is more urgent than that
of returning thanks.

SAINT AMBROSE

Thanksgiving is the end of all human conduct,
whether observed in words or works.

J. B. LIGHTFOOT

Everything God made is good,
and nothing should be refused if
it is accepted with thanks.

1 TIMOTHY 4:4 NCV

Character

Endurance produces character,
and character produces hope.

ROMANS 5:4 NRSV

In many schools, the athletic and academic departments routinely compete for school resources. They should be working together in light of the fact students need both healthy bodies and sharp minds to succeed.

Athletic competition builds strong hearts, and teaches young people to endure and push through fatigue. A coach has the opportunity to teach character by setting goals for the team and showing students that by working together, they can win. When those same high standards are transferred to the classroom, a child learns to work hard individually, and with others, to achieve an academic goal.

Whether you are a coach or an academic, ask God to help you work together to build character in your students' lives.

Character—the sum of those qualities that make a man a good man and a woman a good woman.

THEODORE ROOSEVELT

Character is best formed
in the stormy billows of the world.

JOHANN WOLFGANG VON GOETHE

Character is what you are in the dark.

DWIGHT MOODY

God is more concerned about our character
than our comfort. His goal is not to pamper us
physically but to perfect us spiritually.

PAUL W. POWELL

Who is wise and understanding among you?
Let him show by good conduct that his works
are done in the meekness of wisdom.

JAMES 3:13 NKJV

Enthusiasm

Do not lag in zeal, be ardent inspirit, serve the Lord.

When you became a teacher, did you ever imagine you would need a cheerleader? You probably imagined yourself standing in front of your class, cheering on your students to victory. But who is cheering you on?

Think about a football team. Players say a cheering, enthusiastic crowd can give them that extra burst of energy to make a touchdown. Successful teams make it into the final round of play because of their motivation. Their coaches, as well as enthusiastic fans spurred on by the cheerleaders, encourage them to excel.

Everyone needs a cheerleader, and you have one—God! He created you, understands your potential, and is always nearby cheering you on to victory. All you have to do is tune in.

Be not afraid of enthusiasm; you need it;
you can do nothing effectively without it.

FRANÇOIS GUIZOT

Enthusiasm is the element of success
in everything.

BISHOP DOANE

Apathy can only be overcome by enthusiasm,
and enthusiasm can only be aroused by two things;
first an ideal which takes the imagination by
storm, and second, a definite intelligible plan for
carrying that ideal into practice.

ARNOLD JOSEPH TOYNBEE

Enthusiasm makes ordinary people extraordinary.

NORMAN VINCENT PEALE

Your enthusiasm has stirred most of them to action.

2 CORINTHIANS 9:2 NIV

Gentleness

Thy gentleness hath made me great.

PSALM 18:35 KJV

Gentleness and greatness seem worlds apart. Yet those who have achieved lasting greatness have been people with gentle hearts. Gentleness does not equal weakness. It equals strength.

Dr. Martin Luther King Jr. and Mother Teresa achieved greatness, not because of strident words, but because of their gentle spirits. They were people of faith who believed in a God of mercy and grace—a God who loves all people, regardless of their color or circumstances.

When your students reminisce about their school days in years to come, will they remember you as a person of character, who influenced them by your gentle spirit?

Instead of losing, the gentle gain.
Instead of being ripped off and
taken advantage of, they come out ahead!

CHARLES R. SWINDOLL

Feelings are everywhere ... be gentle.

J. MASAI

Power can do by gentleness
what violence fails to accomplish.

LATIN PROVERB

Nothing is so strong as gentleness,
nothing so gentle as real strength.

SAINT FRANCIS DE SALES

Let your gentleness be known to everyone.

PHILIPPIANS 4:5 NRSV

Determination

Do you not know that those who run in a race all run,
but only one receives the prize?
Run in such a way that you may win.

1 CORINTHIANS 9:24 NASB

Runners call it "hitting the wall." In a long endurance race, the body reaches the end of its limits, and every muscle fiber screams to quit. Experienced athletes know you can push through the barrier and gain a second wind to win.

Teaching is a marathon. Like long-distance runners, most teachers "hit the wall" at some point in their careers. But God called you to a higher purpose when He led you into education. He knew it would take determination to stay the course.

When you feel yourself tiring, becoming discouraged, losing steam, read the Scriptures to regain your sense of mission and bolster your determination. Then look to God to give you a second wind to finish your race.

———

A strong will, a settled purpose, an invincible determination can accomplish almost anything.

THOMAS FULLER

Lord, give me the determination
and tenacity of a weed.

MRS. LEON R. WALTERS

The difference between the impossible
and the possible lies in a person's determination.

TOMMY LASORDA

Be like a postage stamp—stick to one thing
until you get there.

JOSH BILLINGS

We must not become tired of doing good. ...
We must not give up.

GALATIANS 6:9 NCV

JOY

*You have let me experience the joys of life and
the exquisite pleasures of your own eternal presence.*
PSALM 16:11 TLB

Does it seem work and family responsibilities have caused you to lose the joy teaching once brought you?

Take your eyes off your problems and your "To-Do List" for a few minutes, and lift them up to God. When you rest in His presence, and meditate on all the good things He's placed in your life, you will begin to experience His joy—a joy that comes from within, not extinguished by external pressures. Soon you will feel your weariness melting away.

Oh, the "To-Do List" will still have to be dealt with. It won't change—but you will. God's joy will provide a sense of renewed enthusiasm as you undertake the tasks before you.

Happiness depends on what happens; joy does not.
OSWALD CHAMBERS

Joy is the most infallible sign of
the presence of God.

LEON BLOY

Life need not be easy to be joyful. Joy is not
the absence of trouble but the presence of Christ.

WILLIAM VAN DER HOVEN

Joy is an unceasing fountain bubbling up in
the heart; a secret spring the world can't see
and doesn't know anything about.

DWIGHT MOODY

*Jesus said, "Ask and you will receive.
And your joy will be the fullest joy."*

JOHN 16:24 NCV

Prayer

My voice shalt thou hear in the morning, O Lord;
in the morning will I direct my prayer unto thee,
and will look up.

PSALM 5:3 KJV

An old adage says a day hemmed in prayer is less likely to unravel. That's true. If you don't think so, imagine yourself walking into the classroom each morning already heavily weighted down with your own troubles. Then you come face to face with your students' issues and troubling circumstances. Add to that administrative mandates and paperwork. By noon, you may be wondering if you can even make it through to the closing bell.

A time of prayer each morning, unloading your cares on God and drawing upon His unlimited resources of wisdom and joy, can significantly lighten your load and give you a lift before you open your classroom door. It's the edge every teacher needs.

Prayer should be the key of the day
and the lock of the night.

THOMAS FULLER

We should speak to God from our own hearts and talk to him as a child talks to his father.

CHARLES HADDON SPURGEON

All who call on God in true faith, earnestly from the heart, will certainly be heard, and will receive what they have asked and desired.

MARTIN LUTHER

Prayer changes things? No! Prayer changes people and people change things.

PAUL TOURNIER

God listens to us every time we ask him.
So we know that he gives us the things
that we ask from him.

1 JOHN 5:15 NCV

Health

*Beloved, I pray that all may go well with you
and that you may be in good health,
just as it is well with your soul.*

3 JOHN 2 NRSV

Every school year brings outbreaks of colds, flu, and a host of viral infections among students and teachers alike. How do you stay healthy when people all around you are coughing and spreading germs?

Maintaining good health depends on many factors—washing your hands often, a balanced diet, getting enough rest, and controlling stress so your immune system works at its optimum. But it also depends on the condition of your soul. When you are spiritually strong, you have a natural joy that boosts your immune system and helps to ward off infection.

Prayer is also an essential aid to good health. Pray for your students and colleagues that this year would be extraordinary—without the usual onslaught of illness.

Our prayers should be for a sound mind in
a healthy body.

JUVENAL

Look at your health; and if you have it,
praise God, and value it
next to a good conscience.

IZAAK WALTON

The one who has health has hope,
and the one who has hope has everything.

ARAB PROVERB

Take care of your health,
that it may serve you to serve God.

SAINT FRANCIS DE SALES

*Do you not know that your body is a temple of
the Holy Spirit within you, which you have from God,
and that you are not your own?*

1 CORINTHIANS 6:19 NRSV

Rest

He said, "My presence shall go with you,
and I will give you rest."

EXODUS 33:14 NASB

*A*re you getting adequate rest during the school year, or are you working relentlessly from early morning into the evening? Are weekends spent grading papers and preparing lesson plans?

God built rest into His creation plan. Throughout the Scriptures, He talks about the need to rest from your labors. He even set the seventh day aside and designated it as a day of rest. He knew the limitations of the human body and that you would need rest for your body, soul, and spirit.

So, be sure to get enough rest in each area. Take a full eight hours of sleep each night for your body, indulge in hobbies to rest your mind, and spend time with God to rejuvenate and renew your spirit.

Life lived amidst tension and busyness needs leisure--leisure that re-creates and renews.

NEIL C. STRAIT

Take rest; a field that has rested
gives a bountiful crop.

OVID

Jesus knows we must come apart and rest a while,
or else we may just plain come apart.

VANCE HAVNER

There is no music in a rest,
but there is the making of music in it.

JOHN RUSKIN

Jesus said, "Come to me, all you that are weary
and carrying heavy burdens, and I will give you rest."
MATTHEW 11:28 NRSV

Love

Though we have never yet seen God,
when we love each other God lives in us
and his love within us grows ever stronger.

1 JOHN 4:12 TLB

No matter where you teach, you have probably discovered many of your students do not have the sense they are loved. Many of them come from homes where strife and instability have created a love vacuum.

You have more to give your students than lessons in grammar and math. You can also be a loving, reassuring voice they hear every day. Over the course of the school year, you can make a real difference in their lives.

Rules about appropriate teacher-student behavior may restrict your use of physical contact, no matter how innocent. But that doesn't mean you can't make a habit of hugging your students with kind words, gentle, reassuring looks, and loving encouragement.

He who is filled with love is filled
with God himself.

SAINT AUGUSTINE OF HIPPO

I have found the paradox that if I love
until it hurts, then there is no hurt,
but only more love.

MOTHER TERESA

Love is the only spiritual power that can
overcome the self-centeredness that is
inherent in being alive.

ARNOLD JOSEPH TOYNBEE

Love, like warmth, should beam forth on
every side and bend to every necessity
of our brethren.

MARTIN LUTHER

Beloved, let us love one another, for love is from God;
and everyone who loves is born of God
and knows God.

1 JOHN 4:7 NASB

Relationships

*Go in peace. We have promised by the Lord
that we will be friends.*

1 SAMUEL 20:42 NCV

At school you may have many acquaintances. But because of time restraints, you may not have been able to develope deeper relationships with your fellow teachers. Ask God to show you individuals who would welcome a friendly relationship. Be warned, that may mean stepping out of your comfort zone.

Rather than focusing on your students or yourself during break time today, encourage your fellow teachers to talk about themselves. Show interest in their personal lives and find out what concerns them. You will almost certainly find a few who are as eager as you are to get to know their coworkers better.

God created you with a longing for relationships with Him and others. What better place to build those than with people who share your passion for teaching.

You can never establish a personal relationship
without opening up your own heart.

PAUL TOURNIER

A relationship is a living thing.
It needs and benefits from the same attention to
detail that an artist lavishes on his art.

DAVID VISCOTT

Always do what you say you are going to do.
It is the glue and fiber that binds
successful relationships.

JEFFRY A. TIMMONS

There is no hope of joy except in
human relations.

SAINT-EXUPÉRY

Friends love through all kinds of weather,
and families stick together in all kinds of trouble.

PROVERBS 17:17 THE MESSAGE

Justice

With righteousness he will judge the needy,
with justice he will give decisions for
the poor of the earth.

ISAIAH 11:4 NIV

America is great because it is a nation built upon the Constitution, which guides and directs the passage of any new laws. This nation has a built-in system of justice, to punish when those laws are broken.

Similarly, God is a God of law and justice. So why is there so much injustice in the world? Innocents suffer and the guilty often go free. While it may not seem God's justice is swift, it is sure. It is based on an eternal timetable.

When you see injustice, speak up, do what you can. When you don't see justice rendered here on Earth, rest in the assurance God will one day set all things right.

If it is thought that justice is with us,
it will give birth to courage.

ELMER DAVIS

Justice is truth in action.

JOSEPH JOUBERT

No human actions ever were intended by
the Maker of men to be guided by balances of
expediency, but by balances of justice.

JOHN RUSKIN

The pearl of justice is found in
the heart of mercy.

SAINT CATHERINE OF SIENA

*See that justice is done, let mercy be your first
concern, and humbly obey your God.*

MICAH 6:8 CEV

Priorities

*The goal of our instruction is love from a pure heart
and a good conscience and a sincere faith.*

1 TIMOTHY 1:5 NASB

Your life is filled with endless possibilities, so you set priorities and vow those things will be the most important in your life. But priorities are sometimes forgotten, as the tyranny of the urgent, or the lure of the moment takes over.

Take a minute to reflect on your priorities: God, your family, your friends, your students, for example. Did you make them your first concern because they clamored for attention? God's priorities always put people and their highest good first. That's the criteria you should use as you set your priorities.

Learn to say no to extracurricular activities when they shortchange the people in your life. Extra money, prestige, and power are not worth the risk of losing those you love.

Do not let the good things in life rob you
of the best things.

BUSTER ROTHMAN

When first things are put first,
second things are not suppressed
but increased.

C. S. LEWIS

Tell me to what you pay attention,
and I will tell you who you are.

JOSÉ ORTEGA Y GASSET

When you put God first, you are establishing
order for everything else in your life.

ANDREA GARNEY

Jesus said, "Put God's kingdom first.
Do what he wants you to do."

MATTHEW 6:33 NIRV

Patience

Convince, rebuke, and encourage,
with the utmost patience in teaching.

2 TIMOTHY 4:2 NRSV

Have you ever prayed, "Lord, give me patience, and give it to me now?" If so, you aren't alone. Sometimes it takes the patience of Job to corral a classroom of unruly students.

Patience is a fruit of the Holy Spirit, given to anyone who asks. But just like edible fruit, it doesn't mature overnight. Just like an overripe grape left behind at harvest, it can rot on the vine. It needs to be picked and eaten for its sweetness to be tasted.

The next time you find yourself losing patience with your students, take a deep breath, and ask God to help you control your temper, so you can discipline with love. Teach your students the consequences of their behavior, and encourage them with patience.

Patience is bitter, but its fruit is sweet.

JEAN-JACQUES ROUSSEAU

Teach us, O Lord, the disciplines of patience,
for to wait is often harder than to work.

PETER MARSHALL

Be patient with everyone, but above all,
with yourself.

SAINT FRANCIS DE SALES

Be patient toward all that is unsolved in
your heart.

DAG HAMMARSKJÖLD

Be patient when trouble comes. Pray at all times.
ROMANS 12:12 NCV

Time

*To every thing there is a season,
and a time to every purpose under the heaven.*

ECCLESIASTES 3:1 KJV

Do you feel like the school year is flying by and there's just not enough time to accomplish all the academic goals you've set? Perhaps an assembly preempts a lesson, or you find it necessary to spend more time on a concept because your students are having trouble understanding it.

Goals are important, but God measures time through the lens of eternity. The extra moments you spend helping your students succeed are not lost. Your job is more than cramming knowledge into their heads. Teaching children to love learning is an investment that will benefit your students every year.

Use time wisely, but relax and know God has given you more than enough time to accomplish His goals for you and your students.

Only eternal values can give meaning to temporal ones. Time must be the servant of eternity.

ERWIN W. LUTZER

Time is given us to use in view of eternity.

AUTHOR UNKNOWN

What is time? Months, years, centuries—
these are but arbitrary and outward signs,
the measure of time, not time itself.
Time is the Life of the soul.

HENRY WADSWORTH LONGFELLOW

Time is not a commodity that can be stored for
future use. It must be invested hour by hour.

THOMAS EDISON

A wise man's heart discerns both time and judgment.

ECCLESIASTES 8:5 NKJV

Faith

Faith is the assurance of things hoped for,
the conviction of things not seen.

HEBREWS 11:1 NASB

*A*re you growing weary and losing faith in your ability to impact the lives of your students? Don't despair. A breakthrough may be just around the corner.

As a teacher, you must have faith you are making a lasting difference in your classroom. It's possible, even probable, you will never see the final results of your work—the fulfillment of your faith. But day after day, year after year, as you pour yourself into a new group of students, praying and believing they will succeed, you are touching their futures.

Today, pray God will strengthen and renew your faith that you are helping your students reach their greatest potential.

Faith is the final meaning of human existence, and the answers to the questions on which all our happiness depends cannot be found in any other way.

THOMAS MERTON

As the flower is before the fruit,
so is faith before good works.

RICHARD WHATELY

The act of faith is more than a bare statement
of belief, it is a turning to the face of
the living God.

CHRISTOPHER BRYANT

Faith is to believe what you do not yet see:
the reward for this faith is to see
what you believe.

SAINT AUGUSTINE OF HIPPO

We walk by faith, not by sight.

2 CORINTHIANS 5:7 NRSV

Peace

*God's peace, which is so great we cannot
understand it, will keep your hearts
and minds in Christ Jesus.*

PHILIPPIANS 4:7 NCV

Peace can be elusive. People everywhere long
for it, work for it, or protest for it. You may
be one of those people—desperate to find peace in
the midst of your high-anxiety school day.

God says in the Scriptures that peace is only
found in Him. It's a direct result of His presence in
your life. No matter what's going on around you, you
can pause for a moment and focus your thoughts on
Him and peace will begin to well up within you.

Practice thinking about God in those brief
quiet moments between classes or at lunchtime.
The more you think about Him, the more His
peace—a supernatural peace that is beyond your
understanding—will permeate your life.

Peace comes not by establishing a calm outward
setting so much as by inwardly surrendering
to whatever the setting.

HUBERT VAN ZELLER

If the basis of peace is God,
the secret of peace is trust.

J. N. FIGGIS

Peace is not the absence of conflict,
but the presence of God no matter
what the conflict.

AUTHOR UNKNOWN

Christ alone can bring lasting peace—
peace with God—peace among men
and nations—and peace within our hearts.

BILLY GRAHAM

You, Lord, give true peace. You give peace to
those who depend on you. You give peace to
those who trust you.

ISAIAH 26:3 NCV

Hope

If we hope for what we do not see,
we wait for it with patience.

ROMANS 8:25 GNT

Are you going through a difficult time as a teacher? Have you lost hope that circumstances will ever change? Hopelessness can rob you of joy and steal each precious moment.

Biblical hope is more than just expectation or a desire something wonderful is waiting around the bend. It is a confident trust God's plans for your life are right and good. When you put your trust in Him, no matter what is happening at the moment, you can look to today and your future with hope, because He is there.

God Himself is your hope in this life, and for all eternity. Place your trust in Him. Confidently step into your future, knowing God will always be with you—no matter what.

There is no medicine like hope, no incentive
so great, and no tonic so powerful
as expectation of something tomorrow.

SAMUEL JOHNSON

There is no better or more blessed bondage
than to be a prisoner of hope.

ROY Z. KEMP

What oxygen is to the lungs,
such is hope for the meaning of life.

HEINRICH EMIL BRUNNER

Do not look to your hope, but to Christ,
the source of your hope.

CHARLES HADDON SPURGEON

May the God of hope fill you with all joy
and peace as you trust in him, so that you may
overflow with hope by the power of the Holy Spirit.

ROMANS 15:13 NIV

Trust

Trust in Him at all times, O people;
pour out your heart before him;
God is a refuge for us.

PSALM 62:8 NRSV

If you have ever been betrayed, and most everyone has been at one time or another, it might be difficult for you to trust others.

There is Someone you can trust completely, Someone who will never betray a confidence, Someone you can be sure is always looking out for your best interests. That Someone is God.

You can tell Him your deepest thoughts and go to Him with your toughest questions. Sometimes His answers might not make sense right away, but trust His wisdom. You will one day see His purpose.

As you learn to trust God, you will find yourself beginning to trust others again, as well. Let Him show you how to open your heart.

I have held many things in my hands,
and I have lost them all; but whatever I have
placed in God's hands, that I still possess.

CORRIE TEN BOOM

Trust the past to God's mercy, the present to
God's love, and the future to God's providence.

SAINT AUGUSTINE OF HIPPO

All I have seen teaches me to trust
the Creator for all I have not seen.

RALPH WALDO EMERSON

Trust in God and you are never to be
confounded in time or in eternity.

DWIGHT MOODY

Trust in the LORD with all your heart,
and lean not on your own understanding.

PROVERBS 3:5 NKJV

Friendship

*Some friends play at friendship but a true friend
sticks closer than one's nearest kin.*

PROVERBS 18:24 NRSV

Peer pressure is a reality of life. As a teacher, you see its effects every day. One of the greatest things you can teach your students is how to be a true friend, and to choose their friends wisely.

Whether you teach elementary, middle school, or high school students, you can work the topic of friendship into your lesson plans. Use classroom opportunities to talk about the consequences of choosing the wrong friends. Offer them examples of famous friendships.

Pray that God will present you with a chance to talk about friendship in an open and honest way. You can make an eternal difference in your students' lives by helping them make good choices.

Be careful of the friends you choose for
you will become like them.

W. CLEMENT STONE

Choose your friends like your books:
few but choice.

AUTHOR UNKNOWN

A true friend unbosoms freely, advises justly,
assists readily, adventures boldly,
takes all patiently, defends courageously,
and continues a friend unchangeably.

WILLIAM PENN

Tell me who your friends are
and I'll tell you who you are.

AUTHOR UNKNOWN

Jesus said, "Greater love has no one than this,
than to lay down one's life for his friends."

JOHN 15:13 NKJV

Strength

The Lord is my strength, my song, and my salvation.
He is my God, and I will praise him.

EXODUS 15:2 TLB

Strength comes in many shapes and sizes. Some teachers are strong communicators. Some are physically strong. Still others may look small on the outside, but stand tall in their convictions. In what ways are you strong? In what ways do you need to be strengthened?

The key to shoring up your weak areas is to draw your strength from God's unlimited resources. You can do that by fortifying yourself through prayer, Bible reading, and practicing the presence of God in your life. The stronger your relationship with God, the stronger and more confident you will feel as you enter your classroom each morning.

As you look to your heavenly Father, you will find you have all the strength you need—and more.

The weaker we feel, the harder we lean on God. And the harder we lean, the stronger we grow.

JONI EARECKSON TADA

The Lord doesn't promise to give us something
to take so we can handle our weary moments. He
promises us himself. That is all.
And that is enough.

CHARLES R. SWINDOLL

They that wait upon the Lord
renew their strength.

LEONARD RAVENHILL

When God is our strength,
it is strength indeed; when our strength is
our own, it is only weakness.

SAINT AUGUSTINE OF HIPPO

Be strong in the Lord and in the power of His might.

EPHESIANS 6:10 NKJV

Motivation

Let the favor of the Lord our God be upon us;
and confirm for us the work of our hands.

Psalm 90:17 NASB

How do you continue to motivate yourself as a teacher when the excitement of your first day in the classroom is past? Teaching is a marathon, not a sprint. It takes endurance to succeed.

God gifted you as a teacher. Whether you teach preschoolers or adults, He knew you would never be able to do this job without Him. Instead of depending on your own abilities, depend on His to motivate you.

Today, ask God to inspire you to be the best possible teacher you can be. Then keep your eyes open for the way He will do it. God may even use the voice of a small child to encourage you.

Motivation determines what you do.
Attitude determines how well you do it.

Lou Holtz

It is not what a man does that determines
whether his work is sacred or secular,
it is why he does it.

A. W. TOZER

God considers not the action,
but the spirit of the action.

PETER ABELARD

God values not your deeds, but how they are
performed; He does not view the fruit,
only the root and core.

ANGELUS SILESIUS

Whatsoever thy hand findeth to do,
do it with thy might.

ECCLESIASTES 9:10 KJV

Integrity

The integrity of the upright guides them.

PROVERBS 11:3 NIV

Sometimes teachers are called to make tough decisions when dealing with students, parents, or colleagues. You may even take some heat when you walk in integrity and refuse to go along with the crowd.

When you let honesty and truthfulness guide you in every situation, you may not always be popular, but God sees your heart and is pleased. Other teachers may take home school supplies or look the other way when they see student infractions in the hallways. But, if you let God's integrity guide you, He will help you make right choices.

Modeling integrity in your school is the right thing to do. Children learn by example. Let God's light shine through you today as you hold tight to your integrity.

There is no such thing as
a minor lapse of integrity.

TOM PETERS

Integrity is the noblest possession.

LATIN PROVERB

Integrity is not a conditional word.
It doesn't blow in the wind or change
with the weather.

JOHN D. MACDONALD

Integrity has no need of rules.

ALBERT CAMUS

Let integrity and uprightness preserve me;
for I wait on thee.

PSALM 25:21 KJV

Contentment

Do you want to be truly rich? You already are
if you are happy and good.

1 T<small>IMOTHY</small> 6:6 TLB

As a teacher, you may never have great wealth or the accolades of millions. But are money and fame that important?

You came into this world with nothing. The only thing you can take with you when you leave is your character, and the knowledge you have followed God's will for your life. You are influencing the decision-makers of the next generation. The students you are molding and shaping today will be the architects, doctors, and politicians of tomorrow.

Ask God to help you find contentment in who you are rather than in what you possess. Ask God to help you realize and appreciate the contribution you are making to the future.

A little is as much as a lot, if it is enough.

S<small>TEVE</small> B<small>ROWN</small>

God is most glorified in us when we are
most satisfied in him.

JOHN PIPER

The utmost we can hope for in this life is
contentment.

JOSEPH ADDISON

The secret of contentment is the realization
that life is a gift, not a right.

AUTHOR UNKNOWN

I have learned to be content with whatever I have.

PHILIPPIANS 4:11 NRSV

Learning

Let the wise also hear and gain in learning,
and the discerning acquire skill.

PROVERBS 1:5 NRSV

As with most teachers, you are probably required to spend part of your summers taking continuing-education courses, staying abreast of the latest discoveries in your field. or studying new teaching techniques. It may seem like you never reach the place where you know enough.

The Scriptures say learning is a lifelong process. No matter how wise or knowledgeable you are, there is always something new to learn. That's what makes life so interesting.

God instilled a love and passion for learning in you; continue to nurture it. Cherish the time you must spend as a student. Look at the experience as an opportunity to become a more effective teacher, and a more knowledgeable you.

In a time of drastic change,
it is the learners who inherit the future.

ERIC HOFFER

Anyone who keeps learning stays young.
The greatest thing in life is to keep
your mind young.

HENRY FORD

Learning is not attained by chance.
It must be sought for with ardor
and attended to with diligence.

ABIGAIL ADAMS

It is what we think we know already
that keeps us from learning.

CLAUDE BERNARD

If you have good sense, instruction will help you to
have even better sense. And if you live right,
education will help you to know even more.

PROVERBS 9:9 CEV

Grace

Grace to you and peace from God our Father,
and the Lord Jesus Christ.

ROMANS 1:7 KJV

Do those around you speak peace into your life? Conversely, do you speak words of grace (unmerited favor) to people you encounter throughout your day? Sometimes the ability to express God in your life can be short-circuited by busyness.

But no matter what, God wants you to know He sends His grace and peace to you. He wishes only the best for you today, even if you're feeling stressed, or too tired to smile. He loves you and wants you to dwell in His peace at all times.

Take a moment today to bless those around you with your words. Find a new way to greet your students and shine with the inner light of Christ.

―――――◇✕◇――――― ―――◇✕◇――― ――◇✕◇――

Grace is love that cares and stoops and rescues.

JOHN STOTT

Grace is always given to those
ready to give thanks for it.

THOMAS À KEMPIS

There is nothing but God's grace.
We walk upon it; we breathe it; we live
and die by it; it makes the nails
and axles of the universe.

ROBERT LOUIS STEVENSON

A state of mind that sees God in
everything is evidence of growth in grace
and a thankful heart.

CHARLES FINNEY

The grace (blessing and favor) of
the Lord Jesus Christ (the Messiah)
be with your spirit.

PHILEMON 1:25 AMP

Compassion

The LORD is gracious and righteous;
our God is full of compassion.

PSALM 116:5 NIV

Do you show compassion for others? Everyone makes mistakes—some silly and some more serious. Your students may blow a test because of carelessness, or a family member may instigate an argument.

Compassion can smooth over the rough places in your relationships. People were drawn to Jesus because He had compassion for them. Every word, every action, was filled with His love and desire to see them cared for. In the same way, God wants you to love others and show compassion when they make mistakes. Your kindness and concern can bring out the best in them.

Today, ask God to give you a compassionate heart. Learn to empathize with those around you.

Anyone can criticize. It takes a true believer
to be compassionate.

ARTHUR H. STAINBACK

When you make that an effort to feel
compassion instead of blame or self-blame,
the heart opens again and continues opening.

SARA PADDISON

The Christian's compassion must be
like God's—unceasing.

WILLIAM BARCLAY

I would rather make mistakes in kindness
and compassion than work miracles
in unkindness and hardness.

MOTHER TERESA

Be kind and compassionate to one another,
forgiving each other,
just as in Christ God forgave you.

EPHESIANS 4:32 NIV

Gifts and Talents

*We have gifts that differ according to
the grace given to us.*

ROMANS 12:6 NCV

There may be many reasons you entered the field of education. But the Scriptures reveal teaching is a gift of God. Yet, someone helped you discover that talent.

Most children eventually ask the questions: "Who am I? Why am I here?" One of the greatest gifts you possess, is the ability to help your students find their life's profession. Is that child in the third row destined to become a computer analyst? Is the one in the last row a writer? Do you have a budding scientist in your classroom?

When you help your students discover their callings in life, and nurture their gifts and talents, you are fulfilling God's gifts, and calling for your own.

Your talent is God's gift to you.
What you do with it is your gift back to God.

LEO BUSCAGLIA

Teach your children to use what talents
they have; the woods would be silent if
no bird sang except those that sing best.

AUTHOR UNKNOWN

Use your gifts faithfully,
and they shall be enlarged.

MATTHEW ARNOLD

All our talents increase in the using,
and every faculty, both good and bad,
strengthens by exercise.

ANNE BRONTË

Like good stewards of the manifold grace of God,
serve one another with whatever gift
each of you has received.

1 PETER 4:10 NRSV

Wealth

To enjoy your work and to accept your lot in life—
that is indeed a gift from God.

ECCLESIASTES 5:19 TLB

Wealth can be measured in many ways. Some people think of it only in terms of riches and possessions, reflecting a popular bumper sticker that reads, "The one with the most toys wins."

As a teacher, unless you marry someone well off or inherit a trust fund or family estate, it is unlikely you will ever live in a mansion or drive expensive cars. But God does not equate wealth with your bank account. Rather, He looks at the abundance of well-being in your heart. If you enjoy and thrive in your work, you have true wealth.

The next time you hear someone bragging about a new "toy," just smile and remember you possess the greatest treasure of all—God's love demonstrated through the gift of teaching.

If you want to feel rich, just count all the things you have that money can't buy.

AUTHOR UNKNOWN

The real measure of our wealth is how much
we'd be worth if we lost all our money.

JOHN HENRY JOWETT

There is nothing wrong with people
possessing riches. The wrong comes when
riches possess people.

BILLY GRAHAM

God only, and not wealth,
maintains the world.

MARTIN LUTHER

Jesus said, "Your heart will always be
where your riches are."

MATTHEW 6:21 GNT

Confidence

In quietness and confidence shall be your strength.
ISAIAH 30:15 KJV

When you think about God, do you see Him as someone to be feared, or do you see Him as a loving, heavenly Father you can approach with confidence?

When children feel loved and valued by their parents, they feel free to crawl up into their parents' laps for fun, comfort, or instruction. You can confidently go to God for the same things, and much more.

If you need grace to make it through the day, forget the "thee's" and "thou's" of a formal prayer. Ask God to give you an image of Him with arms open wide. Now crawl up in His lap and soak up His loving presence. He's waiting for you.

The greater and more persistent your confidence in God, the more abundantly you will receive all that you ask.

ALBERT THE GREAT

Nothing can be done without hope
and confidence.

HELEN KELLER

I place no hope in my strength,
nor in my works:
but all my confidence is in God.

FRANÇOIS RABELAIS

Above all things, never think that you're not
good enough yourself. My belief is that in life
people will take you at your own reckoning.

ANTHONY TROLLOPE

The LORD will be your confidence.

PROVERBS 3:26 NRSV

Future

I know the plans I have for you, says the LORD,
plans for your welfare and not for harm,
to give you a future with hope.

JEREMIAH 29:11 NRSV

What's the attitude of your students about the future? Do they view it through lenses of doom and gloom? Or, do they dream about their prospects for a bright tomorrow?

As a teacher, you have great influence over the children in your classroom. Yes, they may hear about war and famine, a sagging economy, or a thousand unjust acts. But you have the opportunity to instill hope in them, despite their circumstances or the latest headlines.

Use today's news to discuss the consequences of choices. Give your students hope they can overcome any obstacle and fulfill their dreams.

The only light on the future is faith.

THEODOR HOECKER

Never be afraid to trust an unknown future
to a known God.

CORRIE TEN BOOM

The future is God's: which means that,
wherever the individual being goes—
in life or death—God is there.

HANS KÜNG

The future is as bright as the promises of God.

ADONIRAM JUDSON

Jesus said, "Give your entire attention to what
God is doing right now, and don't get worked up
about what may or may not happen tomorrow."

MATTHEW 6:34 THE MESSAGE

Blessings

Bless the LORD, *O my soul: and all that is within me,*
bless his holy name.

PSALM 103:1 KJV

When someone sneezes, you say, "God bless
you." When you pray over a meal, you
say, "Lord, bless this food." When you attend church,
your pastor or priest may end the service with a
blessing based on Numbers 6:25, "May the Lord bless
you and keep you."

The blessings of God flow out to His children
because of His great love. God wants you to pass
on His blessings by loving others. Without saying a
word, you can bless your students with a smile or a
look of encouragement.

But don't forget those spoken blessings. When
you stand before your students today, speak words of
blessing over their lives. Then witness the positive
impact your words have on those under your care.

The best things are nearest; breath in your nostrils,
light in your eyes, flowers at your feet, duties at
your hand, the path of God just before you.

ROBERT LOUIS STEVENSON

The more we count the blessings we have,
the less we crave the luxuries we haven't.

WILLIAM ARTHUR WARD

God is more anxious to bestow his blessings on
us than we are to receive them.

SAINT AUGUSTINE OF HIPPO

Reflect upon your present blessings, of which
every man has many, not on your past
misfortunes, of which all men have some.

CHARLES DICKENS

*The LORD bless you and keep you; the LORD make
his face to shine upon you, and be gracious to you;
the LORD lift up his countenance upon you,
and give you peace.*

NUMBER 6:24–26 NRSV

Loyalty

*Remember now, O Lord, I pray, how I have walked
before You in truth and with a loyal heart,
and have done what is good in Your sight.*

Isaiah 38:3 NKJV

Sometimes being loyal to God's principles is difficult, especially when others around you find loyalty old-fashioned. You may hear people say, for example, that the administration isn't loyal to its teachers, so why should we be loyal to the school?

But, loyalty is never out of fashion, and there are many ways you can exhibit allegiance to God in your daily life. Be dependable and reliable. Be a person who can be counted on to do what you've promised. Others will notice your constancy, whether it's showing up for a faculty meeting or handing in reports on time.

Show your loyalty to God and all He stands for by being His ambassador at your school. Exhibit His traits of trustworthiness and steadfastness.

Our loyalty is due not to our species but to God.

C. S. Lewis

Loyalty means that I share a common ideal
with you and regardless of minor differences
we fight for it, shoulder to shoulder,
confident in one another's good faith,
trust, constancy, and affection.

KARL MENNINGER

There is nothing so loyal as love.

ALICE CARY

Unless you can find some sort of loyalty,
you cannot find unity and peace in
your active living.

JOSIAH ROYCE

By loyalty and faithfulness iniquity is atoned for,
and by the fear of the LORD one avoids evil.

PROVERBS 16:6 NRSV

Mercy

Hear my prayer, O LORD; listen to my cry for mercy.
PSALM 86:6 NIV

Have you ever said something you regretted the moment it popped out of your mouth? Perhaps it was in the heat of an argument at home, or when you were under stress at school. What you said might have been unintentional, but it still hurt someone.

God understands. No one is perfect. He knows that you are human. Prayer offers you the solace you seek. You can't take back the words, but you can ask God for mercy, before you offer an apology to the person you hurt.

Model God's mercy in your classroom. Teach your students how to admit to mistakes by admitting your own. When you apologize for hurting someone with your words, your students will learn to extend mercy to others.

Mercy is compassion in action.
AUTHOR UNKNOWN

Nothing graces the Christian soul
as much as mercy.

SAINT AMBROSE

He who demands mercy and shows none ruins
the bridge over which he himself is to pass.

THOMAS ADAMS

Two works of mercy set a man free: forgive
and you will be forgiven,
and give and you will receive.

SAINT AUGUSTINE OF HIPPO

*Surely goodness and mercy shall follow me all
the days of my life: and I will dwell in
the house of the LORD for ever.*

PSALM 23:6 KJV

Security

Peace be within your walls,
and security within your towers.

PSALM 122:7 NRSV

*A*re you afraid of what is happening in the world and feel like it is spiraling into chaos? If you study history, you will find that every generation has faced similar challenges.

When you trust in God, you are assured that no matter what happens, He is with you. He sends His angels to stand guard over you. Even in the midst of chaos, God can bring peace and order to your heart.

Children need to feel secure, and you can give them that feeling of security by putting world events into perspective, reassuring them they are safe. Tell them you and the other teachers in school will watch over them. Today, look to God to help you make your classroom a secure place.

Security is not the absence of danger,
but the presence of God,
no matter what the danger.

AUTHOR UNKNOWN

In God's faithfulness lies eternal security.

CORRIE TEN BOOM

The saints in heaven are happier
but no more secure than are true believers
here in this world.

LORAINE BOETHNER

No matter what may be the test,
God will take care of you.

C. D. MARTIN

They that trust in the LORD shall be as mount Zion,
which cannot be removed, but abideth for ever.

PSALM 125:1 KJV

God's Faithfulness

You, O Lord, are a God merciful and gracious,
slow to anger and abounding in steadfast love
and faithfulness.

PSALM 86:15 NRSV

Are you uncertain about God's faithfulness? Do you wonder if He will abandon you in the midst of a difficult situation like some people have said?

It says in Scripture that God will never leave you, nor will He forsake you. He is always faithful. You can be certain He will keep His promises to you, because His nature forbids Him to lie. No matter what circumstances you find yourself in, God is right there with you.

When you feel battered on every side by your life, your work, your family, or your friends, call out to God. As certainly as He hears your voice, He will respond by drawing close. You can count on it.

God is faithful, and if we serve him faithfully,
he will provide for our needs.

SAINT RICHARD OF CHICHESTER

What more powerful consideration can be
thought on to make us true to God,
than the faithfulness and truth of God to us?

WILLIAM GURNALL

In God's faithfulness lies eternal security.

CORRIE TEN BOOM

Though men are false, God is faithful.

MATTHEW HENRY

*God is faithful; by him you were called into
the fellowship of his Son, Jesus Christ our Lord.*

1 CORINTHIANS 1:9 NRSV

Thoughts

When my anxious thoughts multiply within me,
Your consolations delight my soul.

PSALM 94:19 NASB

Do your thoughts spin around in your head like a hamster on a wheel? Do you long for peace and rest in your mind and thoughts? Are you plagued with unanswered questions about your life and the lives of those around you?

If so, take a deep breath and turn your attention to God. Scripture says you should be anxious about nothing, because God knows what you need. When you think about the vastness of God's creation and His great love for you, it will help put your thoughts into perspective.

Let God fill your mind with His thoughts. Doing so will leave little room for fussing and worrying over things which are out of your control.

Change your thoughts and you change your world.

NORMAN VINCENT PEALE

It concerns us to keep a strict guard upon
our thoughts, because God takes
particular notice of them.

MATTHEW HENRY

Keep your thoughts right, for as you think,
so are you.

HENRY H. BUCKLEY

Think positively and masterfully,
with confidence and faith, and life becomes
more secure, more fraught with action,
richer in achievement and experience.

EDDIE RICKENBACKER

Keep your minds on whatever is true, pure, right,
holy, friendly, and proper. Don't ever stop thinking
about what is truly worthwhile and worthy of praise.

PHILIPPIANS 4:8 CEV

Eternal Life

*This is the way to have eternal life—by knowing you,
the only true God, and Jesus Christ,
the one you sent to earth!*

JOHN 17:3 TLB

In quiet moments, or in the dark of night, you may have thought about where you will spend eternity. Life is finite. There is no way of knowing how long you have on this earth to fulfill God's purpose.

The Old Testament speaks of life as a mere breath. In the New Testament, Jesus spoke many times about the fact He came to Earth not to condemn the world, but to save it. He died in order that He could prepare an everlasting home for you.

Rest assured that if you put your trust in God and His Son Jesus Christ, you have eternal life. Be comforted today in knowing when you take your last breath in this life, you will take your next in heaven.

Eternity to the godly is a day that has no sunset.

THOMAS WATSON

People who dwell in God dwell in
the Eternal Now.

MEISTER ECKHART

Eternity is the place where questions
and answers become one.

ELI WIESSEL

The life of faith does not earn eternal life;
it is eternal life. And Christ is its vehicle.

WILLIAM TEMPLE

Whoever believes in the Son has eternal life.

JOHN 3:36 NRSV

Forgiveness

*He has rescued us from the power of darkness and
transferred us into the kingdom of his beloved Son,
in whom we have redemption, the forgiveness of sins.*

COLOSSIANS 1:13–14 NRSV

A re you holding a grudge against someone
at school? Maybe they said or did something
you just can't seem to forget or forgive. The incident
keeps replaying in your head over and over again.

You may never quite forget it. But God calls
you to forgive the one who offended you. He knows
when you harbor anger and unforgiveness, it destroys
you, not the one it is directed against. The offender
may not even remember the circumstances that have
become so important to you. In addition, holding a
grudge saps your energy and inspiration. It simply
isn't worth it—on any level.

Pray God will help you to forgive, and bring
you peace of mind.

To forgive is to set a prisoner free
and discover the prisoner was you.

AUTHOR UNKNOWN

Forgiveness means letting go of the past.

GERALD JAMPOLSKY

Forgiveness is God's command.

MARTIN LUTHER

Forgiveness is the key that unlocks the door of
resentment and the handcuffs of hate.
It is a power that breaks the chains of
bitterness and the shackles of selfishness.

CORRIE TEN BOOM

Be gentle and ready to forgive; never hold grudges.
Remember, the Lord forgave you,
so you must forgive others.

COLOSSIANS 3:13 TLB

Life

Jesus said, "I came to give life—life in all its fullness."
JOHN 10:10 NCV

Are you excited about your life as a teacher? Do you have a sparkle in your eyes? A spring in your step?

When you love what you do, you should feel excitement about what the day will bring. God gave you life to enjoy in all its richness. It's not even a choice between seeing a glass half empty or half full. God wants you to fill it to the brim with His abundant life. Try a new teaching method. Adopt an attitude of adventure.

Most of all, ask God to help you make a change that will result in a renewed sense of wonder about the job you've been called to do. Vow to live with *joie de vivre*.

—————

Life is a great big canvas;
throw all the paint on it you can.

DANNY KAYE

I will not just live my life.
I will not just spend my life.
I will invest my life.

HELEN KELLER

Let God have your life;
he can do more with it than you can.

DWIGHT MOODY

The value of life lies not in the length of days,
but in the use we make of them.

MICHEL DE MONTAIGNE

He that findeth his life shall lose it:
and he that loseth his life for my sake shall find it.

MATTHEW 10:39 KJV

Success

O LORD, we beseech you, give us success!
PSALM 118:25 NRSV

Success can mean many things to many people. For some, it means financial prosperity. For others, it may mean job satisfaction, successful relationships, or a secure future. How do you measure success?

In the daily flurry of teaching, interacting with students, and grading papers, it is easy to forget to ask for God's help in all you do. Yet Scripture says He is the One who will bring success to your life.

Start by thanking God for the good things He has brought into your life: for family, friends, and your career. Then ask Him for help in making today successful in His eyes. There is no greater satisfaction than knowing your success is pleasing to God.

I have only to be true to the highest I know—
success or failure is in the hands of God.
E. STANLEY JONES

He has achieved success who has lived well,
laughed often, and loved much.

BESSIE ANDERSON STANLEY

Success is a journey, not a destination.

BEN SWEETLAND

It is not your business to succeed,
but to do right; when you have done so,
the rest lies with God.

C. S. LEWIS

*It is not that we think we can do anything of
lasting value by ourselves. Our only power
and success come from God.*

2 CORINTHIANS 3:5 NLT

Scripture

He [Jesus] opened their understanding,
that they might comprehend the Scriptures.

LUKE 24:45 NKJV

Theologians, academics, and religious leaders have studied and debated the Scriptures for thousands of years. So how, you may be asking yourself, can you a regular person, be expected to understand them? It may not be as difficult as you think.

New translations written in simple language abound. If you start with a Bible written for children, it will help you understand the main stories. There are also study Bibles with notes that can put things into perspective for you.

God wants you to seek Him and know Him. That's exactly why the Scriptures were given. Ask Him to enlighten your mind as you read. If you feel you need extra clarification and insight, you might try asking your pastor or priest.

God did not write a book and send it by messenger
to be read at a distance by unaided minds.
He spoke a Book and lives in His spoken words,
constantly speaking His words and causing
the power of them to persist across the years.

A. W. TOZER

The Bible is God's chart for you to steer by,
to keep you from the bottom of the sea, and to
show you where the harbor is, and how to reach it
without running on rocks and bars.

HENRY WARD BEECHER

When you read God's word, you must
constantly be saying to yourself,
"It is talking to me, and about me."

SØREN KIERKEGAARD

When you have read the Bible, you will know it
is the word of God, because you will have
found it the key to your own heart,
your own happiness and your duty.

WOODROW WILSON

*Using the Scriptures, the person who serves God
will be ready and will have everything he needs
to do every good work.*

2 TIMOTHY 3:17 NCV

Responsibility

Each of us will be accountable to God.
ROMANS 14:12 NRSV

Do you ever find yourself questioning whether you are strong enough or capable enough to walk into a classroom each day and impart wisdom and knowledge to your students?

As a teacher, God has placed a great responsibility in your hands, but you have been prepared for it. All through your childhood and young adult years, like a potter with fresh clay on the wheel, He molded and shaped your character, equipping you for the challenge. Now He trusts you to help mold and shape the character of others.

You have a responsibility to yourself and to God to be the best teacher you can possibly be, but you don't have to do it alone. Today, pray that God will show you how to prepare your students for the paths they will walk tomorrow.

Hold yourself responsible for a higher standard than anybody else expects of you.
HENRY WARD BEECHER

Responsibility is the thing people dread
most of all. Yet it is the one thing in
the world that develops us, gives our
manhood or womanhood fibre.

FRANK CRANE

Action springs not from thought,
but from a readiness for responsibility.

DIETRICH BONHOEFFER

I believe that every right implies
a responsibility.

JOHN D. ROCKEFELLER JR.

*Jesus said, "Everyone who has been given much
will be responsible for much."*

LUKE 12:48 NCV

Comfort

Now let your lovingkindness comfort me,
just as you promised.

PSALM 119:76 TLB

Teaching can be rough. Sometimes it feels like you can't go on one more day. By the end of the school year, you may be as bruised and battle-scarred as a soldier in the field. But don't despair!

God loves you. He knows you grow weary. His desire is to comfort you, to take the load off your shoulders, to put His arm around you, and remind you that your diligence and dedication are pleasing to Him.

Open the Bible and read the beautiful words of the Twenty-third Psalm. They were written for you just as they were written for all those who turn to God for comfort. Imagine Him speaking the words directly to you—because He is.

No affliction nor temptation, no guilt nor power of sin, no wounded spirit nor terrified conscience, should induce us to despair of help and comfort from God!

THOMAS SCOTT

In Christ the heart of the Father is revealed,
the higher comfort there cannot be
than to rest in the father's heart.

ANDREW MURRAY

God does not comfort us to make us
comfortable, but to make us comforters.

ABRAHAM LINCOLN

It will greatly comfort you if you can see
God's hand in both your losses
and your crosses.

CHARLES HADDON SPURGEON

Whenever I am anxious and worried,
you comfort me and make me glad.

PSALM 94:19 GNT

Satisfaction

That everyone may eat and drink,
and find satisfaction in all his toil—
this is the gift of God.

ECCLESIASTES 3:13 NIV

Are you dissatisfied with your life as a teacher? Do you feel discouraged because you never quite meet the standards you've established for yourself? Is there always something more you want to accomplish?

God wants you to find satisfaction in the work He has given you to do. If you are feeling discontented with yourself, perhaps you need to step back and get a fresh perspective. Acknowledge your accomplishments. If there are areas in which you can continue to grow, make note of them, but don't dwell on your inadequacies. Change your techniques slowly.

Find satisfaction and enjoyment in that which you have done well, knowing God loves you and is pleased with you.

The world without Christ will not satisfy the soul.

THOMAS BROOKS

Do not give your heart to that
which does not satisfy your heart.

ABBA POEMEN

People who wait around for life to supply
their satisfaction usually find
boredom instead.

WILLIAM MENNINGER

Look at a day when you are supremely satisfied
at the end. It's not a day when you lounge
around doing nothing. It's when you've had
everything to do, and you've done it.

MARGARET THATCHER

I will satisfy the weary, and all who are
faint I will replenish.

JEREMIAH 31:25 NRSV

Courage

*Jesus said, "In the world you have tribulation,
but take courage; I have overcome the world."*

JOHN 16:33 NASB

Teaching is not for the weak or fainthearted.
It takes courage to face the challenges in
your classroom every day—challenges that have
grown more violent and inexplicable in recent years.
Elementary teachers report aggressive behavior in
kindergartners; and many middle school, high
school, and college teachers cope with hostile
students every day.

But all through the Scriptures God says, "Fear
not." He goes before you and sends His angels to
watch over you. There's even a popular bumper
sticker that says, "There is nothing that you and
God can't handle together."

When you pray, ask God to grant you the
courage and the wisdom to deal with any situation
that might arise in your school.

———◦◦◦◦◦——— ———◦◦◦◦◦——— ———◦◦◦◦◦———

Courage is fear that has said its prayers.

DOROTHY BERNARD

Courage is doing what you're afraid to do.

EDDIE RICKENBACHER

Have plenty of courage; God is stronger than the Devil. We are on the wining side.

JOHN WILBUR CHAPMAN

Courage consists, not in blindly overlooking danger, but in seeing and conquering it!

JEAN PAUL RICHTER

Be strong and of a good courage; be not afraid, neither be thou dismayed: for the LORD thy God is with thee whithersoever thou goest.

JOSHUA 1:9 KJV

Expectancy

Jesus said, "Be ready all the time.
For I, the Messiah, will come when least expected."
LUKE 12:40 TLB

When a woman finds out she is pregnant, she is filled with expectancy. She prepares a nursery and plans for the baby's delivery. Likewise, before walking down the aisle, a bride plans her wedding down to the smallest detail. Her heart races when at last she looks into her bridegroom's eyes at the altar.

Are you expectant? The Scriptures promise that Christ will return someday to gather up His own. No one knows exactly when that day will be, but we are to live as if He will come any moment.

Today, think about how you will feel when you are face to face with Jesus, gazing into His eyes. Are you ready?

High expectations are the key to everything.
SAM WALTON

We block Christ's advance in our lives
by failure of expectation.

WILLIAM TEMPLE

There is something new every day if
you look for it.

HANNAH HURNARD

The quality of our expectations determines
the quality of our action.

ANDRÉ GODIN

In the morning, O LORD, you hear my voice;
in the morning I lay my requests before you
and wait in expectation.

PSALM 5:3 NIV

Humility

*Be clothed with humility: for God resisteth the proud,
and giveth grace to the humble.*

1 PETER 5:5 KJV

What kind of teachers do you admire? Those who are always pushing themselves forward for attention? Or those who go quietly about their day, satisfied in the knowledge they are doing their jobs well?

Some think being humble means being weak. But the truth is, someone with an unassuming nature knows deep inside they have great abilities, and they strive to be the best they can be.

True humility is a character trait of God. He certainly has reason to exalt His accomplishments and remind us of how powerful He is. But instead, He focuses on His children—loving, caring for, encouraging them.

Are there teachers in your school who exhibit humility? Show your appreciation by letting them know how valuable they are to your team.

Humility is nothing else but a true knowledge
and awareness of oneself as one really is.

THE CLOUD OF UNKNOWING

For those who would learn God's ways,
humility is the first thing,
humility is the second,
humility is the third.

SAINT AUGUSTINE OF HIPPO

If you are humble, nothing will touch you,
neither praise nor disgrace,
because you know what you are.

MOTHER TERESA

It is no great thing to be humble when
you are brought low; but to be humble when
you are praised is a great and rare attainment.

BERNARD OF CLAIRVAUX

Humble yourselves in the sight of the Lord,
and He will lift you up.

JAMES 4:10 NKJV

Generosity

*You will be enriched in every way for
your great generosity.*

2 CORINTHIANS 9:11 NRSV

The Scriptures point out it is more blessed to give than to receive, that God rewards a generous heart. Generosity doesn't always come naturally, however. Most of the time it must be taught. That means you will have to look to God to help you nudge your students toward generosity, both by instruction and example.

The best way to do that is to point out simple, spontaneous acts of generosity in the classroom. Encourage your students to always give more than is expected, whether that means time, effort, or material goods. Most importantly, demonstrate generosity in their presence.

Look for opportunities to teach your students a principle that will bring them blessing and good will for the rest of their lives.

———◇◆◇——— ———◇◆◇——— ———◇◆◇———

You are never more like God than when you give.

AUTHOR UNKNOWN

Life begets life. Energy begets energy.
It is by spending oneself that one
becomes rich.

SARAH BERNHARDT

He who gives what he would as readily throw
away, gives without generosity;
for the essence of generosity is in
self-sacrifice.

SIR HENRY TAYLOR

You do not have to be rich to be generous.
If he has the spirit of true generosity,
a pauper can give like a prince.

CORRINE U. WELLS.

A generous person will be enriched.

PROVERBS 11:25 NRSV

Decisions

Choose life and not death!

2 Kings 18:32 NIV

Not every choice you make in life will be momentous or have eternal consequences. But every decision contributes to your character. Like a stalactite formed over time by the steady dripping of water, you become the individual you are by your daily actions.

When you use God's standard for making decisions, you will become more like Him with each passing day. How can you know God's character? Read the Scriptures. By studying His love letter written to you, you will better understand God's nature, and begin to make the right choices.

Put God's Scriptures into your heart. When you face a tough decision, you will have a powerful resource to help you make it a good one.

———◇※◇——— ———◇※◇——— ———◇※◇———

God always gives his very best to those
who leave the choice with him.

James Hudson Taylor

O Lord, may I be directed what to do
and what to leave undone.

ELIZABETH FRY

Living is a constant process of deciding
what we are going to do.

JOSÉ ORTEGA Y GASSET

Destiny is not a matter of chance,
it is a matter of choice.

WILLIAM JENNINGS BRYAN

Choose life, that both you
and your descendants may live.

DEUTERONOMY 30:19 NKJV

Meditation

Whatever is true, whatever is honorable, whatever is right, whatever is pure, whatever is lovely, whatever is of good repute, if there is any excellence and if anything worthy of praise, let your mind dwell on these things.

PHILIPPIANS 4:8 NASB

Physically, you are what you eat. Spiritually, you are what you think. If you worry and stew over a situation, looking for your own answers about how to fix a problem, peace will elude you.

Instead, when something is bothering you, meditate on the nature of God. He has all the answers. Take a moment to think about His greatness. Then, think about what is right in the world, rather than what is wrong with it. Contemplate a Scripture and let its words wash through your mind.

Meditation is about pausing in the midst of your situation and listening to the inner voice of the Holy Spirit. It's like a calmness break, designed to give you an opportunity to focus on the One who has the answers.

Those who draw water from the wellspring of meditation know that God dwells close to their hearts.

TOYOHIKO KAGAWA

Meditation is the activity of calling to mind,
and thinking over, and dwelling on, and applying
to oneself, the various things that one knows
about the works and ways and purposes
and promises of God.

J. I. PACKER

Let us leave the surface and,
without leaving the world, plunge into God.

TEILHARD DE CHARDIN

In the rush and noise of life, as you have
intervals, step home within yourselves and be still.
Wait upon God, and feel his good presence; this
will carry you evenly through your day's business.

WILLIAM PENN

Let the words of my mouth and the meditation of
my heart be acceptable in Your sight,
O LORD, my strength and my Redeemer.

PSALM 19:14 NKJV

Goodness

According to thy mercy remember thou me for thy goodness' sake, O LORD.

PSALM 25:7 KJV

Most adults have done something in their youth they regret. Likewise, some of the children you see before you in your classroom may be labeled troublemakers because of their behavior.

But God sees the heart. Because of His goodness, He can reach out and rescue even the most difficult or disadvantaged child. It may not seem as if you are making a difference. It may not seem as if the child is paying any attention at all. But your words and conduct will be remembered in later years.

Inspire your students with your goodness and your mercy. When you do, you will be reflecting the very nature of God.

God is all that is good, in my sight, and the goodness that everything has is his.

JULIAN OF NORWICH

God's goodness is the root of all goodness;
and our goodness, if we have any,
springs out of his goodness

WILLIAM TYNDALE

The goodness of God knows how to use our
disordered wishes and actions, often lovingly
turning them to our advantage while always
preserving the beauty of his order.

SAINT BERNARD OF CLAIRVAUX

Think of how good God is! He gives us
the physical, mental, and spiritual ability
to work in his kingdom, and then
he rewards us for doing it!

ERWIN W. LUTZER

O taste and see that the LORD is good;
happy are those who take refuge in him.

PSALM 34:8 NRSV

Protection

Lord, you bless those who do what is right.
You protect them like a soldier's shield.

PSALM 5:12 NCV

Are you often afraid? Today's world can be a scary place. It seems as though every day brings news of terrorist attacks, street rioting, or school violence.

But you must not live your life behind locked doors physically, or mentally. Instead, trust in God who promises to provide security to those who call on His name—to make you feel safe even in troubled times. Listen for the quiet, still voice of God alerting you to take shelter in Him when danger is near. Let Him be your armor and shield.

Rest securely in God's protection each day as you continue to do your job and live your life to the fullest.

———✦——— ———✦——— ———✦———

Security is not the absence of danger,
but the presence of God,
no matter what the danger.

AUTHOR UNKNOWN

Prayer is the key that shuts us up under
his protection and safeguard.

JACQUES ELLUL

Safe am I. Safe am I, in the hollow of His hand.

OLD SUNDAY-SCHOOL SONG

Those who walk in God's shadow are
not shaken by the storm.

ANDREA GARNEY

The LORD will keep you from all evil; he will keep
your life. The LORD will keep your going out
and your coming in from this time on
and forevermore.

PSALM 121:7–8 NRSV

Encouragement

Patience and encouragement come from God.
ROMANS 15:5 NCV

Does it seem like you spend your days encouraging your students, but when you need a lift, no one is there to pat you on the back and say, "Good job"?

When you're feeling discouraged and need someone to reach down and lift you up, spend time with God in prayer. Receive encouragement as you cultivate your relationship with Him. His Holy Spirit will sustain and validate you when no one else is around. God's very presence will give you the support you need.

The Scriptures are also a source of encouragement available to you. The Book of Psalms is filled with words of promise and encouragement. Reach out to God. He's waiting to say, "Well done."

Encouragement is oxygen to the soul.
GEORGE M. ADAMS

More people fail for lack of encouragement
than for any other reason.

AUTHOR UNKNOWN

If you wish to be disappointed, look to others.
If you wish to be downhearted, look to yourself.
If you wish to be encouraged,
look upon Jesus Christ.

ERICH SAUER

Encouragement costs you nothing to give,
but it is priceless to receive.

AUTHOR UNKNOWN

If one has the gift of encouraging others,
he should encourage.

ROMANS 12:8 NCV

Identity

Put on the new man which was created according to God, in true righteousness and holiness.

EPHESIANS 4:24 NKJV

In today's high-tech society, your identity can be stolen by thieves who use your Social Security number to obtain a new driver's license and credit cards. It can be difficult to repair the damage.

But no one can rob your identity in Christ. When you seek God and put your trust in Him, He will transform your character and personality, developing within you qualities no thief can steal. You are one of a kind; you cannot be duplicated.

Today, ask God to show you how to become more like Him. Let your identity come from who you are in Christ, rather than from your material possessions, your looks, or what other people say about you.

Everything is good when it leaves
the Creator's hands.

JEAN-JACQUES ROUSSEAU

Is it a small thing in your eyes to be loved by
God—to be the son, the spouse, the love,
the delight of the King of glory?

RICHARD BAXTER

He who counts the stars and calls them by
their names is in no danger of forgetting
His own children.

CHARLES HADDON SPURGEON

The way in which we think of ourselves
has everything to do with how
our world sees us.

ARLENE RAVEN

Be imitators of God as dear children.

EPHESIANS 5:1 NKJV

God's Forgiveness

*You are a God of forgiveness, gracious
and compassionate, slow to anger,
and abounding in lovingkindness.*

NEHEMIAH 9:17 NASB

Do you feel God could never forgive you for the things you have done in your life? Be assured there is nothing you could do God cannot forgive. He sees and knows every one of your thoughts, words, and deeds. He saw them before you were born.

That's why He sent His Son Jesus to carry all your sins and misdeeds to the cross, where they would be atoned for once, and for all. The payment for your debt was so great, it covers the very worst human nature can conceive.

Today, receive God's loving forgiveness for your sins and missteps. Let Him wash you white as snow on the inside. Then go and be a better person for Him.

There is only one person God cannot forgive:
the one who refuses to come to him
for forgiveness.

AUTHOR UNKNOWN

Forgiveness does not mean the cancellation of
all consequences of wrongdoing. It means
the refusal on God's part to let our guilty
past affect His relationship with us.

AUTHOR UNKNOWN

I think that if God forgives us,
we must forgive ourselves.

C. S. LEWIS

The most marvelous ingredient in
the forgiveness of God is that he also forgets—
the one thing a human being can never do.

OSWALD CHAMBERS

You, Lord, are good, and ready to forgive.

PSALM 86:5 NKJV

Honesty

The Lord wants honest balances and scales to be used.
He wants all weights to be honest.

PROVERBS 16:11 NCV

Situational ethics have become acceptable in American society. There are those who say dishonesty in private life does not affect the honesty of public life. Children are learning it is OK to do something wrong, as long as they don't get caught.

But God's standards are unchangeable. All the weights and balances He uses to judge a situation are perfect. Teaching your students to be honest and to tell the truth is a goal worthy of pursuing. Think of ways to emphasize the virtues of honesty, and the consequences of dishonesty, in your classroom.

God has entrusted you with the citizens of tomorrow, those who will establish the moral values of the nation. What an opportunity! Be sure to take advantage of it.

Honesty is the first chapter in the book of wisdom.

THOMAS JEFFERSON

Honesty has a beautiful and refreshing
simplicity about it. No ulterior motives.
No hidden meanings.

CHARLES R. SWINDOLL

I consider the most enviable of all titles,
the character of an honest man.

GEORGE WASHINGTON

If we be honest with ourselves,
we shall be honest with each other.

GEORGE MACDONALD

An honest answer is as pleasing as a kiss on the lips.
PROVERBS 24:26 NCV

Perseverance

Suffering produces perseverance; perseverance,
character; and character, hope.

ROMANS 5:3–4 NIV

Children find it difficult to wait for anything. They live in a world of microwave popcorn, instant soup, and cartoon networks.

Yet, as an adult, you know the enduring things of life seldom come without delay, hard work, and perseverance. Your education took years of study. Your profession involves much daily preparation. You have learned that molding your students is a long-term commitment.

Ask God to show you creative ways to teach your students how to persevere in the face of adversity. As life becomes more challenging, they will be inclined to push through to victory, to keep going until they have fulfilled the destiny for which they were created.

Permanence, perseverance, and persistence in
spite of all obstacles, discouragements,
and impossibilities: It is this, that in all things
distinguishes the strong soul from the weak.

SIR FRANCIS DRAKE

There must be a beginning to any great matter,
but the continuing to the end until it
be thoroughly finished yields the true glory.

THOMAS CARLYLE

Great works are performed, not by strength,
but by perseverance.

SAMUEL JOHNSON

Energy and persistence conquer all things.

BENJAMIN FRANKLIN

You must hold on, so you can do what God wants
and receive what he has promised.

HEBREWS 10:36 NCV

Faithfulness

Trust in the LORD and do good; dwell in the land and cultivate faithfulness.

PSALM 37:3 NASB

After spending time with you, would others describe you as a faithful person? Are you committed to the teaching profession and your students? Do you go the extra mile to give of yourself?

Faithfulness is a trait that must be developed, one faithful act at a time. Take those papers sitting in front of you, for example. What if you don't finish grading them tonight? After all, you've had a long day and your students won't care. But they will notice, and eventually, so will your colleagues.

God is faithful. He requires you to show faithfulness in all He's given you to accomplish. Exercise discipline and foster a faithful point of view. The extra effort will be pleasing to God.

Faithfulness in little things is a big thing.

SAINT JOHN CHRYSOSTOM

We know that our rewards depend not on
the job itself but on the faithfulness
with which we serve God.

JOHN PAUL I

God did not call us to be successful,
but to be faithful.

MOTHER TERESA

He does most in God's great world who
does his best in his own little world.

THOMAS JEFFERSON

Do not let loyalty and faithfulness forsake you;
bind them around your neck, write them on
the tablet of your heart.

PROVERBS 3:3 NRSV

Kindness

*Since you have been chosen by God who has given you
this new kind of life, and because of his deep love
and concern for you, you should practice
tenderhearted mercy and kindness to others.*

COLOSSIANS 3:12 TLB

Are you afraid of losing control of your
classroom if you show mercy and kindness
to your students? The prevailing wisdom is that
unless you stand your ground, students will take
advantage of you.

Being kind does not mean you allow students
to roll over you. Your students need consistent
correction, but it should be a discipline born of
love, rather than fear. It is more kind to reprimand
an unruly student, than it is to allow behavior that
will have a negative impact on the child's life in
the future.

Today, pray God will bring peace to your
classroom, and show you how to model kindness,
even in the discipline of your students.

Be the living expression of God's kindness:
kindness in your face, kindness in your eyes,
kindness in your smile, kindness in
your warm greeting.

MOTHER TERESA

A kind heart is a fountain of gladness,
making everything in its vicinity
freshen into smiles.

WASHINGTON IRVING

Constant kindness can accomplish much.
As the sun makes ice melt, kindness causes
misunderstanding, mistrust and hostility
to evaporate.

ALBERT SCHWEITZER

Be kind. Remember that everyone you meet is
fighting a hard battle.

HARRY THOMPSON

Love is kind.

1 CORINTHIANS 13:4 NRSV

Guidance

Where there is no counsel, the people fall;
but in the multitude of counselors there is safety.

PROVERBS 11:14 NKJV

Children need wise counselors, especially when they reach high school. Guidance counselors help them choose the right academic paths to achieve their goals. Are you trying to make an important decision without getting expert advice?

According to the Scriptures, everyone needs sound direction—even teachers. Perhaps you have a personal problem that needs attention, or there is a situation at school you don't know how to handle. Are you trying to solve it yourself? God is always available to give you the right answer, but He may give you advice through another person.

Today, pray God will lead you and give you wise advisers to help you decide the right course of action.

I know not the way God leads me,
but well do I know my Guide.

MARTIN LUTHER

Deep in your heart it is not guidance that you
want as much as a guide.

JOHN WHITE

The teacher of teachers, gives his guidance
noiselessly. I have never heard him speak, and yet
I know that he is within me. At every moment
he instructs me and guides me. And whenever
I am in need of it, he enlightens me afresh.

THERESE OF LISIEUX

When we fail to wait prayerfully for God's
guidance and strength, we are saying with our
actions, if not our lips, that we do not need him.

CHARLES HUMMEL

*If I take the wings of the morning, and dwell in
the uttermost parts of the sea,
even there Your hand shall lead me.*

PSALM 139:9–10 NKJV

Fun

To everything there is a season, a time for every purpose under heaven: a time to weep, and a time to laugh; a time to mourn, and a time to dance.

ECCLESIASTES 3:1, 4 NKJV

Teaching is a gift—a demanding one—that carries an enormous burden of responsibility. But even so, doing what you've been gifted to do should also be fun.

God approves when you include laughter and play in your school day. There may be times when it's appropriate to orchestrate games and other activities. But when you're heart and mind are open to it, fun usually just happens, pulling its power from the moment.

Your classroom need not be a somber place where learning is viewed only as serious business. A little spontaneous fun often stimulates interest and builds a connection between teacher and students. It also relieves tension and stress. So lighten up. Have some fun. There is great joy in fulfilling your destiny.

People rarely succeed unless they have fun in what they are doing.

DALE CARNEGIE

Whence comes this idea that if what we are
doing is fun, it can't be God's will?

CATHERINE MARSHALL

The normal person living to age 70 has
613,200 hours of life. This is too long
a period not to have fun.

AUTHOR UNKNOWN

Perhaps imagination is only
intelligence having fun.

GEORGE SCIALABRA

Our mouth was filled with laughter,
and our tongue with singing.

PSALM 126:2 NKJV

Preparation

As a teacher, you have an incredible opportunity to touch the lives of your students. That means that you must prepare for each new class, not only concerning lesson plans and goals, but also in regard to attitudes toward those God has entrusted to you.

Before you take one step into your classroom, ask God to prepare your heart. Thank Him for each name on your class roster, and ask Him to give you a special love and insight into each individual—regardless of personality and aptitude.

God took care to prepare for His interaction with you. Follow His example as you prepare for your role with each of your students. For some, you may be the only demonstration of God's love in their lives.

The way from God to a human heart is
through a human heart.

SAMUEL GORDON

Don't judge each day by the harvest you reap,
but by the seeds you plant.

CORNELIUS STAM

The greatest mission field we face is not in
some faraway land. It's barely across the street—
our children and neighbors.

DWIGHT OZARD

God's love never imposes itself.
It has to be discovered and welcomed.

BROTHER ROGER

*God our Savior ... desires everyone to be saved
and to come to the knowledge of the truth.*
1 TIMOTHY 2:3–4 NRSV

Topical Index

Blessings	92
Character	32
Comfort	116
Compassion	82
Confidence	88
Contentment	76
Courage	120
Decisions	128
Determination	38
Encouragement	136
Enthusiasm	34
Eternal Life	104
Expectancy	122
Faith	60
Faithfulness	146
Finances	12
Forgiveness	106
Fresh Start	26
Friendship	68
Fun	152
Future	90
Generosity	126
Gentleness	36
Gifts and Talents	84

Goals	16
God's Faithfulness	100
God's Forgiveness	140
God's Love	10
Goodness	132
Grace	80
Growth	20
Guidance	150
Health	44
Honesty	142
Hope	64
Humility	124
Humor	18
Identity	138
Integrity	74
Joy	40
Justice	52
Kindness	148
Learning	78
Life	108
Love	48
Loyalty	94
Meditation	130
Mercy	96
Motivation	72
Nature	28

Patience	56
Peace	62
Perseverance	144
Prayer	42
Preparation	154
Priorities	54
Protection	134
Relationships	50
Responsibility	114
Rest	46
Satisfaction	118
Scripture	112
Security	98
Speech	22
Strength	70
Success	110
Thankfulness	30
Thoughts	102
Time	58
Trust	66
Wealth	86
Wisdom	14
Work	24

Additional copies of this book and other titles
from ELM HILL BOOKS are available
from your local bookstore.

Other titles in this series:

God's Daily Answer
God's Daily Answer for Women